I'm Sorry I Ate Your Favorite Child

CHAPTER ONE: NEVER TAKE FARTING FOR GRANTED

There are a lot of things we take for granted in life. A lot of these things can be unexpectedly convenient. For example, catching the plague can get you out of that dreaded history test. A carbon monoxide leak can get you a free hospital breakfast. And farting, as revolting as it may be, can literally save your life.

I would know. My days are limited, which is why I'm rushing to write this before I die.

My name is Rose Dilfinski. I'm eighteen years old, a senior at Delaware High School. Now, I know Delaware is a relatively small state, but it does have more than one high school. The one I attend just happens to be named Delaware High School. I guess the ancient Delawarians ran out of creative juice. Or important dead people to name a school after.

Anyway, dying at eighteen isn't exactly anybody's dream, but I guess like the plague I mentioned before, it does get me out of my final exams. And at least now I don't have to worry about what I'm going to do after high school. That's one perk of dying. But how exactly did I come about to be dying, you ask?

Well, it's not like I did it on purpose. I mean, I guess I did eat a lot of fart-creating foods. I love ice cream… who doesn't? And I *hate* vegetables, but somehow broccoli passes the taste test, so it's kind of the only one I eat, which means I eat a lot of it. But what does eating fart-creating foods have to do with my premature death, you deliberate?

Let's start at the beginning. God said, "LET THERE BE LIGHT…"

Okay, okay. We won't go that far back.

I first noticed how bloated I felt last week, when I got out of bed and began walking like a drunken pregnant cowboy, clutching my stomach and moaning all the way. My twin sister Lily asked me why I was acting more normal than usual and stated that it was freaking her out, my younger brother Jabril told me I was *killing* the Drunken Pregnant Cowboy dance move and asked me if I wanted to star in his next music video, and my grandfather told me to quit "pissin' and moanin' and pass the freakin' marmalade".

It only got worse from there. Sometimes, the pain was so bad I felt like I was being punched or even stabbed from the inside out. Eventually, I began taking medicine and the pain faded away. But I did notice one thing — no matter the medicine, no matter what I ate or drank, no matter how much yoga or power-walking I attempted, I could not fart.

I haven't farted in a week.

Due to the intensity of my pain, Lily ordered me to go to the doctor. We went together, partially because we wanted to get ice cream after, but mostly because Lily knows I hate going to the doctor and I wouldn't go unless she forced me.

I knew it was bad when I saw the grave expression on Dr. Filth's face after I explained my dilemma. He pressed my stomach, took my temperature, and tapped my knee with a hammer. Then he looked down, sucking in a deep breath.

"Rose," he said. "You have Flatulentitis."

Lily gasped and covered her mouth. But I didn't understand.

"Flatulentitis?" I repeated. "What's that?"

Lily shook her head, staring at the floor and blinking back tears.

Dr. Filth sighed. "It means… it means… it means you will never be able to fart again." He reached out and took my hand. "Rose, you know what that means, don't you?"

Lily nodded, tears streaming down her face, but I still didn't get it.

"No. What does it mean?"

Dr. Filth sighed again. "If you can't fart, Rose, the gases build up inside your body until you explode."

"Explode?" I echoed hollowly.

"Your days are limited, Rose. I'm so sorry. There's nothing I can do. There's nothing anyone can do."

"Wait," I said. "How do you get this ailment? Does it spread through farts?"

"No, Rose," Lily interjected, in her best "well-duh" voice, despite the tears streaking down her cheeks. "You *can't* fart."

"So how did I get this?" I asked. "What happened?"

"Consider it a blend of fart-inducing diet and cosmic bad luck," whispered Dr. Filth. With a final sigh, he swept out of the room, leaving my sister and me alone with our thoughts.

"Oh, Dr. Filth!" I called after him, unsure if he could hear. "Since I'm dying and I'll probably never see you again, I'm sorry about that time I tried to convince you I had mad cow disease so you'd give me opiates!"

There was no response. But my conscience felt a lot cleaner regardless.

"Are you okay?" asked Lily, taking my arm.

Surprisingly, I was. I had just been told I was going to die, but I felt emotionally no different than I had moments before. In fact, I was excited about that ice cream we were going to get, even if I knew it would make my gas buildup worse. That was when I realized I had no idea how long it would take the gas to build up to the point where I exploded.

"Lily," I said, turning toward her. "If I explode on you and you end up covered in my guts and bacteria…"

"Clone you?" she guessed, reading my mind.

I grinned. "Exactly."

CHAPTER TWO: WHEN YOU FALTER
AT THE ALTAR

My priest, Father Patrick Armando Gurtierrez, went through a few phases during the twelve years I'd attended his church. When I was a very young child, he was in his later twenties and wanted to be called "Daddy Pat". He dressed like a mix of an Irish leprechaun and a rap star. A few years later, it was "Father P", and he wore a pair of wraparound sunglasses while carrying a skateboard everywhere he went, even in the building. Now he's "Papa P-Rick", and he dresses like a normal priest in a pair of normal boring glasses, plain shoes, and that weird robe thing. But his hair is dyed electric blue and styled like Elvis, so he hasn't completely lost his touch.

A couple days after Lily and I went to the doctor and received my deadly diagnosis, our family crammed into our bright orange van and headed to church. The rest of the family didn't know about my diagnosis yet, but Lily had promised to pray extra hard for me that Sunday.

"I'll even ask Papa P-Rick to pray for you if you want," she suggested.

"That's okay," I said. "He kind of scares me."

Anyway, our family had been picked to do that thing where you carry gifts up to the altar or whatever it's called. I was bringing up the rear, next to Lily, when suddenly she gasped and slapped my arm.

"Girl, what are you doing? You're offering a gift at the altar!" she hissed.

"Um… so are you?"

"Isn't there that Bible verse that says you should leave your gift and go settle your disputes before offering the gift at the altar?"

I frowned. "Why do I have to do that but you don't?"

"Because you're dying and I *ain't*, girlfriend. You gotta settle all your disputes with anyone and everyone you ever quarreled with. Otherwise, you'll go to hell. You don't have much time left to convince God you're heaven material. Better get all the brownie points you can."

She was right. And so, I placed my gift down on the floor and sprinted out of the church.

My family, who had been walking ahead of Lily and me, didn't even notice. But they would hear about it, no doubt. Every other head in the church turned to watch me bolt out the doors, Lily rolling her eyes and shaking her head like she wasn't the idiot who started it all.

CHAPTER THREE: THE WEIRDEST FAMILY EVER

After I sprinted out of the church that day, intending to settle my disputes, I realized I had no idea how to do that. I knew there were people I had wronged in my life, but I'm not exactly the most diplomatic person there is, which is probably why I wronged those people in the first place. Fortunately, Lily promised to help me.

The two of us decided to hold a family meeting. Not to inform them of my illness, because for some reason we couldn't explain, we felt that was a bad idea. Instead, we wanted to let them know we would be taking some time to travel and wouldn't be home for a few days or even a couple weeks… however long it would take me to die. I didn't want to explode at home, because then I'd have to haunt the house when I died, and that would probably traumatize the rest of the family. So Lily and I decided we would stay in a hotel, leaving our room only to settle my disputes with those I had quarreled with, and traumatize the hotel's housekeepers instead.

Before I describe the family meeting, I suppose I should introduce you to the rest of my family.

WARNING: Contains nuts, and may be toxic.

GRAMPS

Gramps is ninety-seven years old, which probably explains why he's always so grumpy. (Lily and I used to call him Grumps behind his back.) His first name is Samuel. He moved to the United States from Jamaica when he was a child, and sometimes you can hear a hint of his childhood Jamaican accent. He hates everyone, he hates everything, and to be honest with you? I think he hates himself.

He uses a yellow SpongeBob walker to get around, which was a joke Christmas gift from Lily and me years ago after his old walker broke. He hated it, as predicted, and tried to throw it away, but Mom threatened to throw him out of the house if he didn't thank us and use it.

Mom is his only child, and his wife, our grandmother, died almost twenty years ago. So perhaps loneliness is also a contributing factor to his grumpiness. I mean, there are like nine of us stuffed into this house, but Gramps has never exactly been the kind of grandparent to get warm and fuzzy with his grandchildren… or even talk to them, other than to scoff or sneer. He gets the best bedroom in the house, on the ground floor because of his walker, and spends most of his time locked inside, yelling at his TV or an annoying fly or dog-walkers out the window.

DAD

Deonte Dilfinski is probably the normalest out of all of us. He works as a banker, Monday through Friday, nine to five like a typical American citizen. He wears a nice suit, glasses that are ordinary but somehow not boring, and his hair is shaved close to his head. He's the kind of guy you would see in the background of movie scenes, just a regular guy who smiles when you pass him on the sidewalk, then checks his watch and crosses the street to head to work, completely minding his own business. When he comes home, he helps arrange dinner, helps with the dishes, then heads to the living room to watch the news. Then he reads a book until he falls asleep in his chair.

As normal as you can get, right? Sometimes I wonder if he was secretly a terrorist or a mobster or something in his past life, and that's why he got punished with a horrifying family like the rest of us.

MOM

Mom, Tatiana Dilfinski, is a real estate agent. That always sounded like an easygoing job to me, but as soon as she gets home from a showing or something, she bursts into Rant Mode, where her voice goes from shrieky loud to whisper quiet several times in the same sentence and her facial expressions become so overly dramatic she looks like a serial killer and her arms go flying all over the place in wild hand gestures. Dad just nods and listens, waiting out the storm until she's done.

Other than that, Mom is pleasant. As long as you don't chew too loudly or walk right past her chair while she's sitting there TRYING TO THINK AND NOW YOU DISRUPTED HER or anything like that.

Yeah. She's a bit volatile. I think she's where the rest of us got our crazy from.

AYESHA

There's always that one family member the rest of you don't talk about, and for us, that's Ayesha. Uttering her name is the equivalent of summoning a demon in our house, because that's what we suspect she is.

Look, I have nothing against crazy people. In fact, I'm a bit crazy myself. But Ayesha is crazy in the bad way, and that's all I want to say about it. For reasons I won't disclose, Mom and Dad used to lock her bedroom door from the outside each night when she went to bed, and the rest of us always jolted awake anytime we heard a creak in the night because we thought it could be her, escaped and roaming the halls with a flaming steak knife or perhaps a bazooka, that manic look in her eye. Then one day, not long after her seventeenth birthday, she disappeared during the night. Mom and Dad found her bedroom window open, curtains flapping in the breeze. It's been five years, and we've never heard from her since.

Let's hope we never do.

LILY

Obviously, you've met my twin sister at this point. We're identical, but she wears her hair in a ponytail and mine is shaved. She's also a bit more athletic than me, and looks nicer and leaner, although she doesn't wear makeup or jewelry like I do. She's far more sarcastic than me, doesn't do as well academically, and also tends not to care what people think about her, which I wish I could do better.

EZEKIEL

Zeke is our sixteen-year-old brother, the nerd/geek/dork/ smart moron of the family. He even wears nerdy circular glasses and wears stripey polo shirts and khakis to school, which he must buy with his own money because Mom refuses to buy them for him — she says they look "preposterous". He's built a few computers and gaming systems in his life, which I guess is something to be proud of. He watches the news with Dad every night, then flips the channel to trivia shows, where he always beats every contestant. Then, as soon as the last trivia show ends, he falls flat on his face on the couch, instantly asleep and snoring obnoxiously.

I don't know how he does it. I'm not sure if I should be jealous or not.

JABRIL

Jabril is our thirteen-year-old brother, an aspiring hip hop dancer. He also got the best looks out of all of us kids, the only one to inherit Mom's pea green eyes. He has dreadlocks, and he's tall and lanky but not too tall or too lanky. He's always smiling, even when Gramps makes fun of him or his dancing.

CLYDE

Clyde is our ten-year-old brother. I don't really know how to describe his personality, because he doesn't really have one. I guess that is his personality. He's the kind of person who does everything like a robot… he wakes up at 6:30 because that's what time the sun is fully up. He only eats healthy and never drinks anything but water or plain milk. He doesn't speak unless it's to say "Excuse me" or answer a question, but the only questions he actually answers are yes or no questions. If you ask his opinion on anything, he doesn't really have one. He comes straight home from school and does his homework, then double checks his answers, then literally STUDIES for hours on end until dinner. Then he goes to sleep, even though it's not even eight o'clock.

ARTHUR

Lily and I share a room, and each of our beds is under a different window. For a few years now, we've noticed Arthur always stares inside Lily's window, staring directly at her until she leaves the room. When she steps outside, he goes away. As soon as she enters the room, he magically appears in the window. How he knows she's coming, I have no idea. We even tested our theory to see if he was watching her by having her pretend to step in and out of the room super fast, and sure enough, each time she started to step outside, he started to go away. Until she quickly stepped back inside, and he stopped himself. She did this several times in quick succession, and he kept her pace perfectly.

It would be creepy if Arthur wasn't a robin. But he's a robin. So we let him stare at Lily through the window all he wants.

And secretly pray he gets eaten by a snake.

So that's my family. As for me, well, it doesn't really matter because I'm dying so you can read my eulogy soon enough. Anyway. Now that you've met everyone? Let's see them in action. Back to the family meeting!

Lily and I stood at the head of our long rectangular table, while our parents, grandparent, and siblings sat staring at us. Finally, Lily cleared her throat, glaring at me sideways.

"Are you going to say anything?" she muttered.

"Me? You're the better speaker!" I muttered back.

"This is *your* predicament."

"You don't have to say it like it's my fault!"

"Girl, you're the one eating broccoli three times a day."

"It's not my fault. It tastes good!"

"It *so does not*. See, this is why you're dying. You ain't worldly enough to survive in this life."

Meanwhile, the rest of the family shuffled awkwardly and attempted to make sense of what little they could hear of our bantering.

Lily sighed. "Fine, I'll do it. Okay, so, the first thing everyone should know is that

EVERYTHING IS OKAY. I repeat, NOBODY
IS DYING. Or anything like that."

Dad raised his eyebrows and nodded.
Mom gave us her best stop-wasting-my-time
expression. Gramps just seemed disappointed
about the nobody dying part.

"But Rose and I have decided we are
going to take a trip," Lily continued, lacing her
arm through mine. "We've booked some time in
a hotel. We will need to miss school for our trip,
but who cares? It's pretty much summer."

Zeke scoffed. "No, it's not."

"Close enough. It's April."

"Lily," I said, chiming in before Zeke got
to be the smart-mouth like usual. "It's October."

"Oh."

Dad leaned forward, a grave look on his
face, and I was worried he was going to say we
couldn't go. But instead, he said, "Make sure
you carry plenty of bear spray in case you run
into Ayesha."

The lights flickered. Thunder crashed.
And every single one of us flinched.

"Deonte," Mom reprimanded. "We don't
say the *A* name in this house."

"Right. Sorry."

"We'll bring garlic to keep her away,"
Lily promised.

CHAPTER FOUR: ARTHUR SHOWED UP OUTSIDE OUR HOTEL WINDOW THIS MORNING AND LILY IS SO FREAKED OUT SHE WANTS TO GET A RESTRAINING ORDER, BUT I DON'T THINK YOU CAN DO THAT WITH A BIRD

So we just closed the curtain and ignored him.

"Think, Rose," said Lily, trying to pretend she wasn't still shaken over her obsessive avian stalker. "You might not have much time. How many people do you need to apologize to? Five hundred thousand? Ninety million?"

"Ninety million? What kind of person do you think I am?"

"Well, how many, then?"

"Two," I declared, with confidence. "I already apologized to Dr. Filth for the mad cow incident, and there are only two other people I've ever wronged in my life."

"That is *soooo* not true."

"You remember Ellie from second grade? And Trayvon from soccer camp?"

"I think so."

"They both live within walking distance of this hotel. It's perfect!"

"Great!" said Lily. "Lead the way."

CHAPTER FIVE: ELLIE FROM SECOND GRADE

"Mom just texted and asked what we were up to," said Lily, as we walked up the sidewalk.

"You didn't tell her the truth, did you?"

"No," said Lily. "Not entirely, anyway. I just told her we were going to visit Ellie From Second Grade. And, hey — are you sure she still lives in the area? I mean, we haven't seen her since *second grade*!"

"She transferred schools in third grade, but she still lives in the area," I promised.

"How do you know?"

"Because Myranda lives four miles away from her, and she can always hear her coughing."

"Oh, that's right. She always was a loud cougher."

We rang the doorbell at Ellie's house, a tiny blue box that literally looks like it only has one room. Ellie's mother answered, wearing a cloth face mask.

"Hi, Mrs. Twintler," greeted Lily, with a smile and a wave. "Is Ellie home?"

"She is. But shouldn't you two be in school?" Mrs. Twintler asked. Her voice was muffled and nasally from the mask. She sounded like that one annoying puppet from that one annoying puppet show.

"Oh, we've got… a free period," said Lily. "Ellie does, too?"

"Oh, no," said Mrs. Twintler, shaking her head. "She's home because she has tuberculosis."

My jaw dropped, but somehow Lily kept it together.

"Ah," she said politely. "I guess we can come back some other time."

"Pff." Mrs. Twintler did that weird dismissive hand gesture thing. "Come on in. She's upstairs in her room. It's no big deal. It's just tuberculosis."

"Right. Just tuberculosis." Lily turned to me, eyes wide.

"Actually, Mrs. Twintler, I think we should go," I interjected.

"You don't have to go," she said, exasperated. "Look, I know tuberculosis gets a bad rap. It's killed a lot of people. But so have donuts and pepperoni pizzas and even cute cuddly kittens! You don't hate donuts and pepperoni pizzas and cute cuddly kittens, do you?"

Lily and I were silent for a long time. I knew she was thinking the same thing I was — we should have expected this. Ellie From Second Grade was always sick with something, and it was never just the flu or the common cold. Our first day of second grade, she went home after lunch because the nurse found out she had rabies. Her first day back after having rabies, she went home within an hour because the nurse diagnosed her with the bubonic plague. I think at one point, she even had a new illness that she got to name herself. So why didn't Lily and I remember this, and pack hazmat suits for the journey?

"I guess we better come in while we can," Lily said finally. "We don't know if we'll be able to come back. You know, with… time running out because of… you know."

I sighed. She was right. I didn't have much time. I couldn't afford to be selfish. What if I didn't get into heaven because I refused to apologize to Ellie?

"Do we need masks, like you?" asked Lily, turning back to Mrs. Twintler.

"Oh, *heavens*, no!" she cried. "I wear this for fun. Come on in."

She held the door and we walked inside. The house was small, but it did indeed have more than one room. We marched up the stairs to Ellie's room. It was easy to find because we followed the sound of yodeling donkeys, which was actually just her coughing. Her door was wide open and she was sitting in the middle of the floor, which was littered with used tissues. She looked exactly as I remembered — curly blond pigtails, round glasses, blue eyes. Her nose was bright red, and her eyes were swollen, but she grinned at us.

Her grin was like that of a serial killer.

"What are you doing?" I asked.

She shrugged. "Just sitting." Her voice was messed up from the illness.

"Just… sitting?"

"God, Rose, don't judge," Lily snapped. "You just sit all the time."

"Yeah, I sit while *doing* something."

"Rose! Don't make things worse. We're here to make them better, remember?"

"Oh. Right."

Ellie scooched forward, interested. "Make things better?"

I quickly stepped backward, imagining tiny tuberculosis germs swimming toward us in the air. Lily rolled her eyes and pushed me back forward.

"Girl, you're dying anyway!" she hissed.

Well, I guess that was true.

"Make things better," Ellie repeated. "What does that mean? Are you doctors? Do you have a cure for tuberculosis?"

"Unfortunately, no."

"Are you another one of those hallucinations I get from my sick meds?"

"No, we're... do you remember us? We're Rose and Lily from second grade," Lily said.

"Rose and Lily From Second Grade! Of course I remember you! I tried *so hard* to give you diphtheria on April Fools' Day, but you just wouldn't take it!"

She burst into a painful-sounding laughter punctuated by coughs.

I opened my mouth, about to apologize for the way I had wronged her, when I became distracted by the bagged loaves of bread all over her room. I mean, literally *all over*. There were bags of bread on the windowsill, on her dresser, in her bed, on the floor...

"Wow, I guess you really like bread," I said, startled.

"Mmm, yeah. It's all right."

"You like the way it smells?" Lily asked.

"No," said Ellie. "I like the way it sounds. Listen."

We stood in complete silence.

Finally, Lily said, "Um… beautiful."

Ellie nodded thoughtfully. "Yeah. I guess it looks good too."

I decided to just spit it out before things got any weirder.

"So, Ellie, I know second grade was a long time ago. But do you remember when I pulled out your chair right before you were going to sit in it and you fell and broke your coccyx? Then when you were in the hospital, I came to bring you a card and I tripped and spilled the hot tea on your bedside all over you and you had to get treated for second-degree burns? Then when you came back to school I walked up to you to apologize but I was sick that day and I ended up barfing all over you as soon as I opened my mouth?"

Ellie frowned at me. "No."

"You… *don't* remember all that?"

"No… I wouldn't remember something as trivial as that! What are you playing at, Rose From Second Grade?"

I stared at her for a minute, unsure if she was joking. But she stared back, looking just as confused. Lily cleared her throat, gesturing for me to wrap things up.

"Um… okay. So you don't remember me breaking one of your bones and giving you second-degree burns and painting you with my stomach acid. But even though you don't remember, I still want to apologize."

Ellie didn't say anything. She just kept giving me her bug-eyed stare.

"Do you forgive me?" I pressed.

"You haven't apologized yet. You merely stated you wanted to."

Gritting my teeth, I managed not to march over and strangle her. "I'm sorry I put you in the hospital twice and yakked on you."

Ellie snorted and did that same weird dismissive hand gesture thing her mom had done. "Whatever. You don't really think I'd care about *that*, do you?"

"Well, uh, yeah. Most people would."

"Most people are weird, Rose From Second Grade. Most people don't like the way bread sounds. They actually pretend *it doesn't have a sound*. Did you know that?"

"Uh…"

"We listened to it just now. Didn't you like the way it sounded?"

"I… yeah…"

"Good. At least you've got one thing going for you."

Lily was trying so hard not to laugh, she looked like she was being electrocuted. I glared at her, and tried to get back on topic.

"So, um, pushing bread sounds aside, I just… I thought apologizing was the right thing to do. The noble thing to do."

Ellie stared at me for a long time. I was worried that maybe she'd gone into a trance. Then she blinked, a slow creepy smile inching across her face. "The noble thing to do? *The noble thing to do?* That's so… heartwarming!"

As Ellie jumped up and ran toward us with her arms outstretched, Lily and I broke multiple world sprinting records to get out of her house.

CHAPTER SIX: TRAYVON FROM SOCCER CAMP

"Well, that was a nightmare," panted Lily, as we finally slowed to a walk after bursting out of Ellie From Second Grade's house. We'd had to run a full mile before the sound of her coughing became quiet enough for us to feel safe.

"Whose idea was this?" I reminded. "You're the one who said I need to apologize to everyone I wronged before I die."

"Well, you're the one who wronged them in the first place!"

"It doesn't matter. We've got the hard apology out of the way. Now we only have one more."

Lily frowned. "Are you sure you only need to apologize to two people? That doesn't seem like very many."

"Lily, I'm as close to perfect as a person can get. I don't make that many mistakes."

"Well... okay," said Lily. Even she couldn't argue with me there. "Who's the next person, again?"

"Trayvon From Soccer Camp. Do you remember him?"

Lily nodded. Since she was more athletic than me, she still played sports and knew where all our school's star athletes lived. She began leading the way to Trayvon's house, which was fortunately in the opposite direction of Ellie's.

A few times, we thought we heard a robin, and Lily dove into the bushes to hide. She'd never seen Arthur while she was outside before, only outside her window, but she was still terrified of the prospect. I mean, he was her stalker, which meant he did have the potential to be dangerous.

"Look, he's outside," I said, pointing to Trayvon's house as I pulled Lily out of the bushes for the thirty-ninth time. An elderly couple looked at her curiously as they passed.

Lily followed the direction I was pointing and saw Trayvon in his driveway, shooting a basketball at the hoop attached to the garage door.

"Oh, good," she said. "If he's as dangerous as Ellie was, at least it'll be easier to escape."

I was sure Trayvon wouldn't be dangerous. I mean, I hadn't seen him since the first and only year I'd ever done soccer camp, fifth grade, which was the same year I realized sports really were not for me. So I guess I didn't really know that much about him. But surely he wouldn't have tuberculosis! Surely we wouldn't have any issues with him like we had with Ellie.

As we got nearer, I noticed he'd grown very tall in the past few years, and he was quite muscular. He wore a baseball shirt, a cap with a football on it, and shorts decorated with little tennis balls. There was even a tattoo on his forearm reading, *I love sports.*

Trayvon turned as we approached, eyeing Lily. She was covered in spare twigs and leaves from diving into the bushes so many times, and her hands and arms were streaked with dirt. But apparently, Trayvon was too polite to say anything about that. He smiled at us.

"What's up?"

"Hi, Trayvon," said Lily, spitting out a small twig. "Do you remember us from soccer camp?"

"No," he said, frowning. "Soccer camp was a million years ago."

"Oh. Well, I'm Lily Dilfinski, and this is my sister Rose. And she owes you an apology."

41

Trayvon raised his eyebrows. "An apology?"

I thought about just turning around and walking away. What was the point of apologizing if he didn't even remember who I was? That meant he didn't remember what I'd done, so if I reminded him, wouldn't I be doing him more harm than good? But what I had done in fifth grade had made him cry, made him *sob*, so hard he'd had to go home early. I heard his mother had to call the school the next day and let them know he wouldn't be in for class because he was still crying so hard that he'd had to go to the hospital for dehydration. I sucked in a deep breath and prepared myself.

"Trayvon," I began. "I am so sorry that I —"

But he had begun running around the driveway, dribbling his ball, pretending to ward off imaginary opponents, faking passes to imaginary teammates, talking like an announcer the entire time.

"It's a tight game, folks! It all comes down to this. He passes, he feints, he's back in possession…"

I watched him dart around the court, paying me no attention at all. Then I turned to Lily, shrugging. Did it count as an apology if he wasn't paying attention? Should I still say what I'd come to say?

She nodded, giving me the stern look an adult gives a child being forced to apologize to another child. I sighed, turning back to Trayvon. He was still running around and dribbling.

"I'm sorry that I —"

"He shoots, he... *Ohhhh,* dang it! Just glances off the rim!"

"I'm sorry for —"

"Final seconds of the game! Neck and neck, but he's got the ball, he's got the skill, does he got the win?"

"I'm sorry I called —"

"HE SHOOTS! HE SCOOOORES! SLAM *DUNK,* FOLKS!"

He began a celebratory dance, then jumped back into action, muttering and faking passes. At this point, I decided to just blurt it out, whether he was listening or not.

"I'm sorry I called sports stupid in fifth grade!"

Trayvon had been about to shoot, but he froze, the ball sliding out of his grip and bouncing off into the bushes.

"T-trayvon?" Lily asked, concerned. "Trayvon...?"

But with a pit in my stomach, I realized what was coming. He'd done the same thing in fifth grade. I had assumed he would have grown out of it by now. But like eating Froot Loops in your underwear, there are just some things you never grow out of.

His face crumpled up and he let out a massive sob. Tears began streaking down his face.

"Rose, what's going on?" Lily demanded.

"Sh-she said," Trayvon sobbed, pointing at me, "sh-sh-she said…"

"I said sports were stupid," I finished for him, and he began sobbing even louder.

"Sports… stupid?" Lily echoed, and Trayvon clapped his hands over his ears.

"Stop, *stop!*"

"Trayvon," said Lily, but apparently she didn't know what to say to him. So she turned and glared at me instead.

"I… I forgot how emotional he gets," I muttered.

Trayvon collapsed on the ground, hugging himself and rocking back and forth as he wailed.

"I can't believe you said that!" he screeched. "Why, oh, *why* would you *say* that!? Oh, I'm going to have nightmares for weeks! I'll have to go back to therapy! *I don't know if I'll ever recover!*"

"Trayvon," I said, squatting next to him. I began to reach out to pat his back, but he flinched away as if my hands were acid. "I'm really sorry. Sports are not stupid."

He recoiled. "Stop! Stop using the *S* word when you talk about sports! Stop!"

"Sports are wonderful," I said. "I just love sports."

"Sports are great," Lily added. "The best thing ever."

"We love sports," I began chanting. "We love sports!"

"Yeah, uh… we love sports," Lily chimed in. "We really love sports!"

"Sports are so wonderful! Sports are so great!"

"Sports, sports, sports! There's nothing better than sports!"

"Yeah, uh… sports, sports, sports! Oh, how we love sports!"

Trayvon managed to push himself back up to his feet and wipe his face on his sleeve.

"You can't just undo something like that. It's not that easy." Shaking his head, he turned on his heel and marched into the house, slamming the door behind him. Through the window, we watched him curl up on the couch, crying into his hands again.

Lily turned back to me, glaring.

"What? I apologized, didn't I?"

"You upset him!"

"I still *apologized*. It's not my fault he didn't accept it."

Lily sighed. "I guess you're right. According to the rules, all you have to do is apologize. It doesn't matter if they forgive you or not. Shall we move on to the next one?"

"The next one?" I asked, as we began up the sidewalk again. "I told you, that was the last one!"

"Rose, there's no way you only ever wronged two people! There must be someone else."

"Nope," I said happily. "I'm all clear! Shall we get one last ice cream before I spontaneously combust?"

CHAPTER SEVEN: THE WISDOM
OF PAPA P-RICK

Lily and I were sitting in the park, enjoying the sunny day and the giant chocolate swirl ice creams we had just bought. I was thinking about how grateful I was to have a clean slate. Now when I died, I'd have nothing standing between me and the gates to heaven! There was nothing else I had to atone for! I was completely sinless. I almost wanted to go ahead and explode right then and there, just to get it over with, and to see the horrified faces of the family enjoying a picnic several feet away. But I didn't get to be happy for very long.

"Rose," said Lily, smacking me on the arm. "Look who it is!"

I turned, finding a man with electric blue hair strolling along the sidewalk, rapping to himself and doing ridiculous dance moves as he walked.

"Papa P-Rick?"

"I've never seen him outside of church before! This is crazy! It feels wrong! It's like… seeing him in his underwear."

I scoffed. "Lily, it's not that big of a deal. It's *nothing* like seeing him in his underwear."

"How do you know? Have you ever seen him in his underwear?"

"Ew, of course not!"

"Hey, it's a valid question," said Lily, looking affronted. "He does underwear modeling on his days off. Hi, Papa P-Rick!"

He stopped, turning to see who had called him. Both of us waved.

"Billy and Bose!" he cried.

"Lily and Rose, Papa P," Lily corrected.

"Oh, right, right." He walked over and sat across from us at our picnic table. "How have you two been? Is everything okay? You went running out of the church like your hair was on fire on Sunday, Fose."

"Rose," I said. "Yeah, everything's fine. Lily and I just got everything taken care of."

"Great!"

"Papa P-Rick, you're going to be so proud," said Lily, leaning forward. "Rose here just went around and apologized to everyone she's ever wronged in her life."

"Really?" He turned to me, looking impressed.

I nodded, swelling with pride.

"What on earth would make you want to do that?"

"She found out she's dying, Papa P," said Lily. "From Flatulentitis."

The priest's face grew sorrowful and sympathetic. "Oh, Gose. I'm so, so sorry."

"Rose," I said. "And it's okay, Papa P-Rick. I'm getting into heaven soon. I'll be living in paradise soon enough."

"Oh, heaven doesn't exist, my dear," said Papa P-Rick, laughing. "That's just something we priests advertise as a way for you to come to our services, so we get paid. *Come to us, and we'll teach you how to earn happily ever after when you die! DON'T come to us, and you burn in hell for eternity!* It's like how doctors invented vaccines to make you think you're building up immunity against an illness, but they're really just injecting you with a super large dose so you'll get sick and have to come back to the doctor so they get paid more. It's like how dentists make your teeth *look* cleaner, but they're actually rubbing bacteria all over them so you'll have more dental problems and have to keep going back. I thought everyone knew that!"

Lily and I exchanged a look, eyes wide.

"Why… why are you a priest if you don't believe in heaven?" I asked.

"Hey, a job's a job, am I right?"

"Yeah, I guess. I guess you're right."

"But I'm still proud of you for going out there and apologizing to everyone you owed an apology," said Papa P-Rick, patting my hand. "At least now you'll feel better going into death. You won't feel guilty. You apologized to all seven people you ever wronged!"

"Seven?" Lily asked.

"Seven?" I repeated.

Papa P-Rick nodded, giving me a knowing look. "You see, my dear, heaven may not be real… but the Lord is. And the Lord tells me that there are seven apologies you've needed to make in your life."

"That's not true!" I snapped.

Papa P-Rick frowned. "Are you questioning the Lord?"

"Of course she's not questioning the Lord!" said Lily, laying a hand on my arm to stop me from jumping up in outrage. "See, Rose, I told you there must be more people you owe an apology to."

"I apologized to three already! Dr. Filth, for trying to get him to give me opiates. Ellie

From Second Grade, for breaking her coccyx and giving her burns and puking all over that new dress she wore that day. Trayvon From Soccer Camp, for calling sports stupid. There can't be more than that!"

Papa P-Rick sighed sympathetically. "Oh, Nose. We all like to think we're more perfect than we really are."

"My name is Rose!" I snarled.

"That's right, Flose."

"Papa P," Lily interjected, before I could throw the rest of my ice cream into his face, "can the Lord tell you who exactly it is that Rose needs to apologize to?"

He gave her a stern look. "Now, Jilly —"

"Lily."

"Villy. I can't give you all the answers. You can't apologize just to clear your name. You have to actually mean it. So you need to take the time to think about who you wronged."

"You hear that, Rose?" Lily demanded, whirling on me. "Take the time to think about it."

"But I don't have much time! I could explode any second now! You know what, I don't care about apologizing anymore! Now that I know heaven doesn't exist, what motivation should I have to make up for everything I did wrong? It won't get me into heaven. What's the point?"

Lily seemed unable to come up with an answer, but Papa P-Rick leaned across the table.

"Tell ya what, Glose."

"Rose."

"Grose. If you apologize, Grose, to every single person you owe an apology to... I will make sure you have the most extravagant funeral this world has ever seen. The pope will come. The President will come. People will be talking about it for centuries."

I was tempted. I liked extravagance. I liked having better things than everyone else. But still, it would require hard work. Was it worth it?

"She'll do it," Lily declared, patting my arm.

I sighed. Now I had to do it, or I'd let Lily and Papa P-Rick down. "Okay. I'll do it."

"Great!" cried Papa P-Rick. "Well, I'll leave you ladies to it. Good day, Snilly and Snose."

He got up and walked away, rapping under his breath and doing his unusual dance moves.

I finished my ice cream and crossed my arms. "So I still owe four people an apology.

Who could it be, Lily? Who could it *possibly* be? I'm an angel!"

The answer hit me like a bucket of cold water thrown into my face. I couldn't believe I hadn't thought of it before.

"Lily! I just remembered! *Myranda, the Girl Who Eats Paste!"*

"What about her?" Lily asked, frowning.

"We were just talking about her, too," I said. "When we were talking about how I knew Ellie still lived in the area, because Myranda could hear her coughing. But I completely forgot about what I did to Myranda!"

"What did you do to Myranda?" Lily asked.

"Well... there's a reason she can hear Ellie coughing four miles away," I explained hesitantly. "And not just because Ellie coughs loud. I mean, that's part of it, but..."

"But what?" Lily pressed, finishing her own ice cream.

"But... Myranda can also hear a lot of things the rest of us don't while we're in our houses, because... well, Myranda doesn't live in a house."

"She lives outside?"

"Um... kind of..."

"What are you talking about, Rose?" Lily demanded, starting to sound annoyed.

I stood up from the table. "Let's just go. It'll be easier to show you than tell you. You'll see."

We started down the sidewalk, headed for Myranda's.

CHAPTER EIGHT: MYRANDA, THE GIRL WHO EATS PASTE

We ended up taking a bus to get to Myranda's, since she lived kind of far. When it dropped us off near a row of houses, Lily started to walk toward them. But I grabbed her arm and steered her in the opposite direction.

"What are we going this way for?" she asked, confused. "There's nothing this way except for an empty field and an old Dumpster."

"You'll see," I muttered, as I dragged her along.

As we got close enough, we could hear banging and rattling from inside the Dumpster. Lily was afraid we were about to be jumped by a gang of vagrant raccoons. But I calmly walked up to the Dumpster, knocked on its side, and waited. The lid sprung open, and out popped the smiling face of our classmate Myranda. There was a rotting banana peel in her red hair.

Lily's jaw dropped. "Myr... Myranda?"

"Hey, guys!" Myranda cried, waving. "So nice of you to come visit! I didn't think you knew where we lived now."

"You… you live… in there?" Lily stammered. Her eyes were so wide she looked like that annoying puppet from that annoying puppet show.

"Yeah, it's a bit tight for all of us, but we make it work," said Myranda, with a shrug. "My siblings live in the right back corner. I get the right front corner. My parents get the entire left side to themselves."

"I… *wow*…" said Lily. She began to slowly back away. I grabbed her arm to keep her beside me.

"I think this is the first time you've seen our new place," Myranda continued. "Care for a tour?"

"You… you want us to go… in there?" asked Lily, looking terrified.

"We'll pass," I said quickly.

"Ya sure? It's not every day you get to tour the home of the future world's most famous singing star!"

"Your home is a Dumpster," whispered Lily. "*Literally.*"

"So, uh, listen," I said, before Myranda could get offended. "There's actually a super important reason we came here today, and it *wasn't* to make fun of your home." I shot Lily a glare.

"Okay. What's up?" asked Myranda. She propped herself against the edge of the Dumpster, smiling. The black banana peel slid out of her hair.

"I just wanted to say," I said, "I'm sorry."

Myranda looked at me blankly. "For what?"

"For… this." I gestured to the Dumpster.

Lily snorted. "Girl, ain't your fault they're living in a Dumpster."

"Actually, it is," I corrected.

"What?" cried Lily.

Myranda laughed. "It's a super funny story. Tell her, Rose!"

I sighed. Lily would never see me the same way again. But I was dying. Maybe she would have mercy on me.

"Last year, I was walking home from a party all by myself. You were at home sick. I was just passing Myranda's old house, walking a little too close to it, I guess. I was trying to light a cigarette. I got dive-bombed by a shrieking crow —"

"What do birds have against our family?" Lily interrupted, obviously thinking of Arthur the robin.

"I jumped in fright, dropping the lighter and the cigarette. I lit Myranda's house on fire."

"What!?"

"And the whole thing burned down!" exclaimed Myranda, chortling with laughter. "It was so funny!"

"Right," said Lily, looking concerned. "Funny…"

"Our insurance was garbage and we couldn't afford a new home. So we had to move in here!" Myranda said, gesturing to the Dumpster. "But really, Rose, you didn't need to apologize for *that.*"

"I… I didn't?"

"Pff! Of course not. The only thing you should be apologizing for is that you didn't invite me to that party you were walking home from. I heard it was *on. Fire!*"

"It was," I admit. "But not as much as your house."

We both burst out laughing, Myranda's plagued with snort after snort. Lily looked at both of us as if worried for our sanity, and as if fearful that our craziness might be contagious.

Finally, Myranda settled down and began eating out of a jar of paste.

"Really, Lily, you can joke about my situation. It's not that bad," she said. "People throw away so many jars of paste that usually aren't even empty."

"Right," said Lily. "I forgot you like eating paste."

"It's great lubricant for my singing voice. Hey! Wanna hear the song I'm working on?"

It would have been rude to say no, so Lily and I both smiled and nodded. Myranda grinned, threw the jar of paste over her shoulder with a loud *ding!* as it landed, and cleared her throat. Then she began to sing.

"She lives in a Dumpster…"

"Where's that music coming from?" Lily whispered, looking around. I shrugged; I could hear the music too, but I had no idea where it was coming from. Myranda kept singing.

"Oh, yeah, she lives in a Dumpster.
So people think she's a grumpster.

61

But living in a Dumpster
Doesn't make you a grumpster!"

The music grew louder. Myranda began dancing in a manner that would make Papa P-Rick proud. Then, to our bewilderment, a group of backup singers popped up from behind her, each covered in garbage but wearing a bright, cheery smile.

"She lives in a Dumpster!" Myranda cried.

("She lives in a Dumpster!") came the backup singers. They were starting to wave their arms, shake their behinds, and even leap from one side of the Dumpster to the other.

"But she is no grumpster!"

("She is no grumpster!") came the backup singers. They began jumping out of the Dumpster and dancing around the outside of it.

*"You don't judge nobody for living
In a Dumpster!"*

*("Don't judge nobody for living in a
Dumpster!")*

*"Because THE WORLD'S BEST SINGER
Lives in a Dumpster!"*

*(The WORLD'S BEST SINGER lives in a
Dumpster!!!")*

The music faded away. Myranda and the
backup singers stood there for a while, their
hands in the air and giant smiles on their faces.
Then the backup singers jumped back into the
Dumpster and disappeared into the filth, while
Myranda stood there leaning against the edge.

"So? What'd you guys think?" she asked,
panting a little.

"Um…" Lily looked at me, eyes wide.

"You have backup singers," I said.
"Impressive."

"You must pay them a lot to live in the garbage with you," muttered Lily, eyebrows raised.

"Oh." Myranda waved her hand dismissively. "They're not getting paid yet. It's just such an honor for them to live alongside the future world's best singer before she's made it yet. I mean, who wouldn't want to do that for me?"

"Right," said Lily. "Who wouldn't?" She gave me a pleading look, clearly wishing to get out of there. I didn't blame her.

"It was a great song," I said. "But we can't stick around any longer. We've got to get going."

Myranda pouted. "You just got here! Sure you don't want to come inside and hang out?"

"We're sure," said Lily, grabbing my arm. "Let's go, Rose."

"See ya, Myranda," I called over my shoulder as we walked away. She disappeared into the garbage, the lid falling shut behind her.

CHAPTER NINE: GURPREET THE WANNABE SHRINK

"That was the most traumatizing thing I've ever endured. The most traumatizing thing I'll *ever* have to endure!" snapped Lily, as we got back on the bus to head back into our side of town. "Including if I have to watch you spontaneously combust!"

But I wasn't listening to her. I stared out the window, watching fields and houses and scenery blur past as the bus bumped along. I had just apologized to my fourth person out of seven, which meant I was over halfway done. That was good. But I had no idea, not even the slightest idea, who the other three people I had wronged were. That was *not* good, because my stomach was starting to feel more bloated and achy, which meant my time was really beginning to run out. I hoped I didn't explode while we were still on the bus. Pieces of me would get all over the floor and seats, and I didn't want to be sat on!

"Are you even listening to me?" Lily demanded.

Apparently, she'd been ranting for several minutes.

"Nope," I said, still staring out the window.

She sighed. "Well, have you at least figured out who the last three people are?"

"Trying to figure it out."

"I wish Papa P-Rick had just *told* us," she fumed. "Surely the Lord knows who you need to forgive. Surely the Lord wouldn't mind Papa P pointing us in the right direction!"

She kept ranting, but I tuned her out again. My eyes had just landed on a familiar-looking house with a familiar-looking yard, right outside the bus stop.

"Gurpreet!" I exclaimed, pointing to the house.

"What?"

"That's the next person I need to apologize to," I said, standing up as the bus stopped at the curb. "Don't you remember when we were walking home from that *other* party last year, the one you went to with me?"

"Yeah," said Lily, standing up and following me off the bus. "You drank so much cherry Kool-Aid you had to stop and pee on the way home. And you were peeing for like seven minutes straight."

"The reason I drank so much was because… well, because cherry Kool-Aid is awesome. But *also* because that was the first party I'd gone to after the one where I burned Myranda's house down," I explained. We sat on a bench and watched the bus peel away. "I was afraid of something like that happening again, so I made sure if it did happen, I had enough water in me to stop the fire."

"So what does you having to stop and pee on the way home from a party have to do with you apologizing to people?" Lily asked.

"Well," I said, my eyes on the familiar-looking house and its familiar-looking yard, "remember how I told you to wait at the corner down there, while I ran back to that gas station over there?" I pointed.

Lily nodded. "Yeah…"

"So… I didn't make it to the gas station," I admitted. "I had to pee *so bad.* I ended up stopping and peeing in that yard, right across the street."

Lily looked at the house and gasped. "Rose, that's Gurpreet the Wannabe Shrink's house!"

"I know," I said, sighing. "I was squatting behind the rosebushes, only my head visible, and he came out and tried to talk to me about how my public urination stunt probably indicated a repressed sense of needing to express myself. But I couldn't hear much of what he was saying because his mother was standing right behind him yelling into her cell phone."

"She called the cops on you?" Lily asked.

"Yeah. She was on the phone with them the whole seven minutes I was at it. *'She's still peeing! She's still peeing! Good Lord, how much can ya pack in one bladder? She's still peeing!'* But I got away before the cops showed up, and Gurpreet mustn't have given her my name. I never got arrested or anything."

"Well, he's a wannabe shrink. He probably *understood* why you did it."

I snorted. "I did it because I could not hold that liquid inside me any longer, *not* because of a repressed need to express myself! But I appreciate him, anyway."

"So you're going to apologize for peeing in his yard?" asked Lily.

I nodded. We stood up and crossed the street, but before we could ring the doorbell, the door opened. Gurpreet the Wannabe Shrink stood there, smiling at us with his usual calm, compassionate facial expression. He wore a blue button-down shirt, like he always wore ever since he decided he wanted to be a shrink.

"Lily and Rose Dilfinski," he said softly, in what one would probably describe as a "shrink voice". "It's so nice of you to stop by."

"Were… were you expecting us?" Lily asked, seeming unnerved by how quickly he had opened the door.

"No," said Gurpreet, still in that peaceful tone of voice. "But I sensed a great bundle of anxious energy standing behind this door, and like a salve to a wound, I found myself drawn. Come, let me whittle away your woes and drown away your doubts." He opened the door wider, gesturing us inside.

Lily and I looked at each other, then stepped into the house.

"Shouldn't you be in school?" Lily asked.

Gurpreet smiled. "Yes, I should," he said serenely. He didn't elaborate.

We followed Gurpreet to his bedroom, which had a sign on the door labeled "*DR. GURPREET'S OFFICE. PROUDLY SERVING THE EMOTIONALLY DISTRAUGHT FOR SEVENTEEN YEARS AND COUNTING*".

"But he's only seventeen years old," Lily whispered.

I didn't respond. I was drinking in
Gurpreet's room. He didn't have a bed. Instead,
he had a large blue sofa facing a large blue
cushy chair. In between the sofa and the chair
was a small table with a basket of fake flowers,
each in a different shade of blue. The walls were
painted blue. In the corner, there was a box of
pillows, each in a different shade of blue. It was
labeled *"CRYING PILLOWS"*.

Following my gaze, Gurpreet picked up a
pillow and held it out to me. "Here. You can hug
this while you cry, if you like."

"Oh, um… thank you, but I'm not here to
cry."

He gave me a sympathetic, yet knowing
look. "That's what they all say. Sit, sit!"

Lily and I sat on the sofa, and he sat
across from us on the couch. He refused to stop
holding out the pillow until I took it, hugging it
awkwardly across my chest. Then he settled his
elbows onto his knees and leaned forward, his
brown eyes full of compassion.

"Now," he said gently, "let it out. It's
okay."

Lily and I exchanged a glance.

"Nobody's judging you," Gurpreet
whispered.

There was an awkward silence as Gurpreet the Wannabe Shrink waited for us to pour out our hearts. Finally, Lily cleared her throat and gave me a very pointed look.

"I think Rose has something she wanted to say to you, Gurpreet."

"Oh?" he asked, turning to me. "Is that true, Rose? What is it? Take your time, of course. Whenever you're ready."

This was stupid. We were wasting time. I just needed to hurry up and spit it out. I cleared my throat.

"Gurpreet," I began. "Do you remember when I —"

"Failed your pre-calculus test?" he asked, in that voice like molten honey. "Yes, Rose, I do. That was just last week, wasn't it? I have to say, I've been expecting this. I knew it would upset you so much."

I gave a derisive snort. "No, of course I don't care about failing that stupid test! I'm here because —"

"Because you were picked last for basketball in gym class last May?" he asked. "I remember that as well, Rose. I remember it just like it was yesterday. I expected you in here much sooner to work on overcoming that horrible display of rejection."

"No, I don't care about that! I'm terrible at sports, everyone knows, it's nothing pers—" I frowned, suddenly feeling a bit uneasy. "Wait. Wait a minute. You weren't in my gym class last year, and you're not in my pre-calculus class right now. How do you know I was picked last for basketball? How do you know I failed that test?"

For a second, Gurpreet's warm smile turned into a smirk. His kind eyes turned sinister. And his sweet voice grew hard. "Oh, we therapists have eyes *everywhere*."

I swear the lights flickered. Lily and I stared at each other, eyes wide, but by the time we looked back at Gurpreet, he was smiling in that soft, gentle way, his eyes radiating peaceful compassion.

"This is why I'm always saying you can't trust therapists," Lily muttered.

I just wanted to get out of there.

"Gurpreet, I'm here because I owe you an apology. I'm sorry about that time I urinated in your lawn."

His dark eyebrows rose. "Ah, yes. *Yes.* I remember that day, as well. I made a report about that in your file."

My heart skipped a beat. "My... my file?"

He chuckled. "Oh, Rose, you know we therapists keep files, don't you?"

"I mean, I thought… you only kept files on your patients. You know, people who… give you *permission* to keep files on them."

Gurpreet smiled and picked up a water glass from the table. Just before he took a sip, he muttered something that sounded like *"permission is overrated"*, but when Lily asked what he'd said, he wiped his mouth, put down the glass, and ignored the question.

"I accept your apology, Rose," he said, reaching out to pat my hand. His hand was ice-cold, and I jerked mine away. "But perhaps we should further discuss your episodes of acting out, to ensure they don't repeat themselves in the future?"

"They won't," I said, standing up and chucking the pillow at him harder than I'd meant to. "We need to go now. Come on, Lily."

She stood up and practically pushed me towards the door, both of us wanting to get out of Gurpreet's bedroom.

"There is one place you run to that will take you nowhere," he called after us. "And that is to run away from your issues!"

"But we're running the heck away from here," Lily muttered, as we tore across his house and tumbled out the front door.

CHAPTER TEN: THE BREAKDOWN

"Is he still in the window?" Lily hissed, as we ducked behind a row of hedges and attempted to army-crawl our way out of sight.

I raised my head just enough to see over the hedge. Gurpreet stood in the window of his house, looking this way and that, but apparently unable to see where we'd gone. He walked away and disappeared farther into the house.

I ducked back under the hedge. "He's gone. But we should still crawl until we're out of sight, just in case."

"Agreed. Why are nice people always the creepiest?"

"Only *fake* nice people are creepy. It's all just an act."

We crawled along the hedges until we were out of sight of Gurpreet's house. Then we straightened up and plopped down on a bench along the sidewalk, watching cars roll by.

We sat in silence for a while. I knew Lily wanted to ask me who the last two people were that I owed an apology, but she seemed too shaken by Gurpreet's creepiness to speak. And as for myself, I was feeling… odd.

I had just seen a young child standing on her porch, hurling eggs at passing cars and laughing like an evil supervillain. My mind flashed back to myself doing that when I was six years old, and how much joy it had brought me, how hard I'd laughed. For some reason, there was suddenly a knot in my stomach, unrelated to my gas. And there were suddenly tears in my eyes, but I was no longer holding a Crying Pillow, so I had nothing to hug to keep the tears at bay.

With an obnoxious honk, I burst into sobs.

Lily jumped, looking at me with a startled expression. "Rose! Are you… are you okay?"

"I… *honk!*... don't want to… *honk, honk!*... die," I wailed, snorting and honking and sobbing myself into a teary, snotty mess.

Lily rubbed my back consolingly. "Oh, Rose. It's okay."

"I'll miss… *honk!*... throwing eggs at cars! I'll miss… *honk, honk!*... laughing at people who step in dog poop! I'll miss… *honk, honk, honk!*... you, Lily!"

Lily wrapped her arms around me, even though I was a disgusting crying disaster. I leaned into her, shaking with sobs.

"If only…*honk!...* if only I'd been able to see the future! If only I'd… *honk, honk, honk!...* known this day was coming. I'd be better prepared!"

"Oh, Rose, you're handling it so well already."

"But I… *honk!...* don't want to handle it! I want to… *honk!...* live!"

"Shhh, honey, it's okay," Lily murmured.

We sat there in silence for a long time, me quaking with tears and Lily silently brushing her own away.

CHAPTER ELEVEN: PAULINE THE FRAUD-INE

When I finally calmed down and told Lily I was ready to reembark on our journey, she told me she'd figured out who one of the last two people I needed to apologize to was.

"Pauline the Fraud-ine," she said, as I dried my face on my sleeve.

I crinkled my nose. "Pauline the Fraud-ine? What'd I ever do to her?"

"Remember when she copied all your answers to that pre-calculus test you failed? Well, it made her end up failing as well."

"Oh, that's right!"

"I remembered just now when you were talking about how you wished you could see the future, so you would have known this day was coming," Lily explained.

"Pauline can't see the future, either," I reminded. "That's why everyone calls her Fraud-ine."

"I know. But it still reminded me of her."

I stood up from the bench, stretching my arms and looking around. "Do you know where she lives?"

"Somewhere in the Chinatown area. It's over this way."

I followed as Lily took the lead. We reached the Chinatown area just as school buses started to pass us, heading to pick up the kids after class. I knew Lily was thinking the same thing I was — the day was drawing to a close. How many days would I have left? But at least I only had two people left to apologize to. Then I'd be ready to die.

Lily, who is quite the stud at foreign languages, asked around in both Mandarin and Cantonese until she found the apartment where the Wangs lived. We stood outside the door, Lily in front in case Pauline's parents answered the door — I wasn't sure how good their English was, and my Chinese was dreadful. But it was the fraud-ine herself who answered the door.

"I foresaw you coming," she said, in a slow, hoarse voice. She stared at us for a long time without blinking, then drew in a breath and continued, "I know exactly what this is about. Oh, yes. Me and my third eye... we know all."

"Then what is this about?" I blurted out, unable to hold it in. Lily tried unsuccessfully to hold in her laughter, turning it into an explosive coughing fit.

"I cannot say aloud; it would disturb the path on which the future has chosen to embark," Pauline drawled.

Lily turned away, unable to hold back another "coughing attack". I somehow managed to keep a straight face.

"Come in, come in," said Pauline. "I have missed you, my dear classmates."

"Why are none of our classmates in school today?" Lily muttered to me as we followed Pauline into the apartment.

"It was destined to be, Lillian," said Pauline, apparently overhearing. "It was written in the stars, you see."

"Oh… right. The *stars*."

"I hear the doubt in your voice. I see the doubt in your mind. But it is irrelevant. The stars will have their way."

"Of course they will," said Lily brightly, plastering a cheerful fake smile onto her face. She gave me her signature "hurry-up" look, but I felt it would be rude to just blurt out my apology, turn around, and leave. We followed Pauline into her bedroom. It was a lot messier than Gurpreet's, with piles of clothes all over the floor, tipped over chairs, and three glaring white cats.

"Do have a seat," purred Pauline, righting a fallen office chair and brushing one of the cats off a stool. It hissed at Lily as she sat where it had been sitting.

I sank into the wheeled office chair, opening my mouth to explain to Pauline why we were there, but she spoke first.

"I can see it all in your face," she droned, as she sat opposite me on her bed. She squinted hard at my face, looking severely constipated. But then she relaxed and nodded. "Oh, yes. Oh, yes. It was as I suspected... but I don't really *suspect* things, you know. I *know*. The third eye, girls. The third eye always knows."

On the bright side, I thought to myself, at least we only have one more of these tirades to sit through after we're done with Pauline.

"It is all upon your forehead, you see," she continued, staring at my forehead in a way that made it awkwardly difficult for me to avoid any type of eye contact. "The forehead tells me..." She sighed. "It tells me... you are not wise."

"But you already knew that, didn't you?" Lily blurted out. "I mean, you copied all her pre-calculus answers, then you both failed that test."

Now it was my turn to hold back a laugh. It's extremely painful to do so when you really, really, really have to fart but you can't.

A flicker of annoyance came over Pauline's face, but she covered it up fast. "Oh, the *test*. Yes, the *test*. I knew we would both fail that test. I knew we would end up with the same answers on every question. But I did not cheat, Rose. I did not cheat from your test."

"Girl, she *saw* you pull it back out of the in-tray after she handed it in," Lily said, apparently having no more self-restraint for the afternoon. "Rose handed in her test, then you plucked it back out of the in-tray when the teacher wasn't looking and copied down all the answers."

Pauline clenched her jaw. "I was merely checking to see that she had finished her test. The stars told me that day would be a *forgetful* day for her. They told me she would be careless and —"

"But why'd you fail the test if the stars tell you everything?" Lily pressed. "Couldn't they tell you all the right answers? Couldn't you *see* the right answers with that fourth eye of yours?"

"It is the *third* eye, Lillian," said Pauline curtly. "And for reasons the stars have chosen to keep from me, I was meant to fail that test. It was —"

"Written in the stars, yeah, yeah, yeah," said Lily, rolling her eyes.

I figured the reason she was being so aggressive was because when Pauline first moved here when we were in fourth grade, Lily was very gullible and immediately believed Pauline when she told everyone she was psychic who could see the future. Pauline then charged whoever was dupable enough twenty-five dollars per reading, and Lily's reading had told her that she would spontaneously turn into a butterfly by the end of the school day.

That was the day Lily stopped believing in psychics. And also the day she became very cautious about spending money.

"Rose came here to tell you something," Lily said, gesturing to me with her head. "But if you already know what it is, we'll just go."

Pauline barely seemed able to restrain herself from glaring at her. "If she came here to say it, she must say it. It is written —"

"In the stars, whatever," snapped Lily. "We get it. Rose? Apology?"

I cleared my throat. "Pauline, I am very sorry that I made you fail your pre-calculus test by giving you the wrong answers even though I didn't give you permission to copy my test in the first place. Please forgive me. Thank you. We'll be going now."

Before Pauline could say anything else, we were hurrying out of her bedroom and had made it out the front door.

"You didn't have to be so rude," I said to Lily, trying not to laugh. "Who knows? Maybe *you'll* wind up with Flatulentitis and you'll have to go around apologizing to everyone!"

"I'm never apologizing to her, even if I'm dying!" Lily sniffed. "She should be apologizing to me about the money she stole from me in fourth grade."

"You mean the money you gave her, idiot."

"Careful, Rose. You only have one person left to apologize to, you can't go around calling people idiots or the list is only going to grow."

"I don't need to apologize to you," I scoffed. "You already forgive me! But now that you mention it... who do you think the last person is?"

We walked out of Chinatown and returned to the bench we'd been sitting at before, neither of us speaking. We were both trying to think of the final person. Obviously, neither of us could come up with anyone.

"Maybe we could call Papa P-Rick and ask him to tell us who the last person is," Lily suggested. "He can't say you haven't been making an effort; you're down to the *last person!* He could give us just one name. It wouldn't hurt."

The more I thought about it, the more I began to wonder if Papa P-Rick was just as fraudulent as Pauline. Did he really know exactly how many people I needed to apologize to, or was he just messing with me? He had admitted he didn't believe in heaven, so maybe he didn't even believe in God. Maybe no Lord had spoken in his ear, told him I needed to apologize to seven people. Maybe there was nobody else!

After all, it would make sense for him to make it up. He had just admitted he didn't believe in heaven and that he was only a priest because "a job is a job". He'd probably let that slip by mistake, and had to cover his fraudulence fast by making it seem like he could speak to the Lord and nobody else could! Otherwise, he would have to risk Lily and me telling everyone that he was a fake, and he'd lose his job!

But just as I turned to Lily, about to share my thoughts on the matter, somebody walked past. My heart sank into my stomach. It was a tall boy our own age, another classmate of ours, headed home from school judging by the backpack he wore. He had curly red hair, rectangular glasses, freckled cheeks, and a cheerful smile. He walked on his toes, which people used to tease him for, but never me. That wasn't what I needed to apologize to him for. What I needed to apologize for had to do with the tiny potted plant he was holding in his hands, cooing and speaking to it while he walked.

And I knew it wasn't going to be an easy apology.

CHAPTER TWELVE: WHEN I ATE BORIS

I met Rock in a botany class we'd been taking junior year. We were table partners, and at first we got along pretty well. I was the only person who didn't tease him for constantly carrying around his favorite plant, a little blueish cactus in an orange and black striped pot. He brought it everywhere, not just botany class — math class. Gym class. He took it to synagogue and shopping and parties! He even took it whenever he went to the bathroom.

"Boris is my favorite," he'd always told me, lightly stroking the cactus. "Boris is that special someone."

Personally, I didn't see what was so great about Boris. But I never meant to kill him.

I had just gotten my wisdom teeth removed, and I was a little dopey from the anesthesia. I'd left school early for the surgery, but realized I'd forgotten my phone in my locker, and there was no way I would ask Lily to get it for me — giving her the combination to my locker was definitely a bad idea, especially so close to April Fools' Day. So I asked my mother to drop me off at the school while she was driving me home, so I could run in and grab my phone from my locker.

Rock wasn't in class for some reason. Class was still going on, and he should have been in botany class at that moment, and I kind of blame him for skipping class. It's kind of his own fault Boris died. But, anyway. I had just rounded the corner to my locker, staggering like a zombie who had just been conked over the head with a giant iron mallet, when I saw Rock sitting at a lunch table nearby. The cafeteria was empty apart from him.

My doped-up brain tried to make sense of what I was seeing. I saw a boy sitting at a lunch table, with a cactus in front of him. My brain said LUNCH TABLE = MEALTIME. STUFF ON TOP OF LUNCH TABLE = FOOD. ROCK = FRIEND. FRIENDS SHARE FOOD.

And so when Rock turned around and smiled at me, I took that as an invitation to share his "food", and I snatched up that cactus and took a large bite. Rock screamed and wailed and grabbed for the plant, but it actually tasted pretty good, so I jerked away and kept eating. I ate the whole cactus, right down until I hit the dirt. Then I handed the pot back, stumbled to my locker, grabbed my phone, and went back outside to where my mother waited in the car. She drove me home and I went to bed, where I slept it off and woke up thinking the whole thing had just been a dream.

I found out the next day that it *had not* been a dream. Rock refused to sit next to me in botany class, and for the rest of the semester he had to sit in the back corner of the classroom on the floor, because there were no other available tables. Someone told me the reason he'd been in the cafeteria the day before instead of in class was because the teacher had finally put her foot down and told him he couldn't keep bringing the cactus to class, and he'd said if his cactus wasn't welcome, neither was he. So he'd gone to sit in the cafeteria with Boris in peace. Only I had shown up and made it not-so-peaceful.

But in the end, I did him a favor, didn't I? He'd only walked out of class because Boris wasn't allowed in the classroom anymore, but after I got rid of Boris for him, he started going back to class and didn't fail. He definitely would have failed otherwise!

Yet Rock didn't see it that way. He refused to speak to me after that, and if we ever made eye contact in the hallway, his face screwed up with such fury that I considered it a miracle his head didn't explode. When I went to him to try to apologize one day, his eyes got all squinty and his voice got all hissy and his fists got all tight and he gritted out, "My plants are my children, *Rose.* And you ate my favorite child."

He never spoke to me again. And I can't blame him for being angry. I'd be angry if someone ate my child, too.

CHAPTER THIRTEEN: APOLOGY ATTEMPT #1

"Oh, that's right! I forgot you did that," said Lily, starting to laugh as I whisper-told the story while Rock disappeared down the sidewalk. "He cried for a week! How'd that thing taste, anyway? Watery? Salty? Like chocolate?"

"Mild," I said. "Kind of like a cucumber. But that doesn't matter. Lily, this is one apology I can't do. I can't do it! He'll never forgive me."

"We established earlier that it doesn't matter if they forgive you or not," Lily replied. "You just have to apologize. That's all you have to do."

"But... but..."

I sighed. Lily was right, but the thing was... I *wanted* Rock to forgive me. I knew I had done him a great personal wrong. I'd killed his best friend. I'd eaten his best friend. I had turned his best friend into my feces and flushed it down a toilet bowl! How do you forgive someone after something like that?

But I wanted him to, more than anything.

"Well," said Lily, after I'd voiced my guilt. "It's been a year, hasn't it? Maybe he's had enough time to grieve. Maybe he'd forgive you now. The only way we'll know is if we try."

She was right. So, neither of us knowing where Rock lived, we stood up and ran down the sidewalk in the direction we'd seen him walking, until we spotted his retreating form in the horizon. Then we creepily followed him at a distance until he disappeared into a big white house at the end of the road.

I stopped where I stood. "Lily, I really don't think I can do this."

I kept seeing Rock's horrified face as I'd devoured his plant. I didn't want to dredge all that up again, for either of us. But Lily grabbed my arm, forced me to walk up to Rock's house, and jabbed her finger into the doorbell.

I held my breath as we waited.

The door creaked open. A man who looked exactly like a thirty-years-older Rock was smiling down at us.

"Hello," he said. "Can I help you?"

I began a series of incomprehensible stammers. The man looked politely confused.

"I'm sorry?" he asked, tilting his head.

Lily rolled her eyes and stepped in front of me. "We're here for Rock," she said.

"Ah," the man replied. "Wait here. I'll see if he's available."

He closed the door. We could hear his footsteps fading away. We stood there a long time before the door opened again. My heart plummeted. But it wasn't Rock. It was his father again.

"I'm very sorry," he said. "Rock isn't in the house right now. You'll have to call again."

And, still smiling, he shut the door in our faces without another word.

Lily and I turned to look at each other.

"He's here," I said. "We both saw him enter this house, didn't we?"

"We did," she confirmed.

"Then why is his dad lying to us?"

Lily sighed. "Rock must have seen us through the window and told his father to tell us he wasn't home."

"I *told* you he wouldn't want to talk to us," I growled.

"He doesn't want to talk to *you*," Lily corrected, smirking.

I glowered at her.

"But we can use that to our advantage," she realized, nodding to herself. "Yeah, we could… we could just wait a little bit, then ring the doorbell again. But it would be just me this time. You could go hide in the bushes or something."

"Hide in the bushes?"

"So he wouldn't see you when he looks out the window. He'd think it was just me, so he would think it's safe to come out and chat," Lily explained.

"Why would he *want* to chat with you, Lily?" I pointed out. "Have you ever even talked to him before in your life?"

"Well… no…"

"Which means he'd know you're here because of something to do with me. Besides, he saw both of us through the window earlier, which means if he sees you're still here, he's going to know I'm still hiding around here somewhere. He's not going to come out and talk to you."

Lily frowned, thinking hard. Then she brightened. "Oh, I've got it!" She reached into her pocket and yanked out a small notepad and pen. Then she handed it to me. "Write him an apology note!"

"But how will I give it to him if he doesn't answer the door?" I demanded.

"You won't. *You* will go hide behind that oak tree while *I* ring the doorbell. Then when *Rock* looks out the window, he'll see *me*, not you."

"But I just told you he's not going to open the door for you because he knows you're here because of me!"

"He might not open the door, but I'm sure his father will," said Lily, grinning. "Then I'll give the note to his father and ask him to pass it along to Rock. Rock will take it because he knows it's from me, not you."

I thought it over. It was worth a try.

"I'm sorry… I ate… your favorite… child," I muttered as I scribbled the words onto the notepad. I handed it back to my sister, with the pen.

She tore the note from the notepad, folded it up, and tucked the notepad and pen back into her pocket. Then she gestured for me to hide behind a large oak tree nearby. I hurried to comply, peeking between two branches as she rang the doorbell. She stood there for a long time before Rock's father answered, his smile now looking a bit strained.

I couldn't hear their exchange. But Rock's father nodded and took the note before closing the door, and my hopes soared. Maybe Rock would forgive me after all! Maybe he would see how desperate I was to apologize, that I was willing to… but the door was opening again, and my thoughts trailed off as my heart began racing. Was it Rock? Would he come outside and declare me forgiven?

No. It was Rock's father. And he was handing something to Lily with a sheepish, almost resigned expression. As she held out her hand for it, he opened his fist, and out fluttered several tiny scraps of paper… Rock's response to my note was to rip it into shreds. All was definitely not forgiven.

CHAPTER FOURTEEN: APOLOGY ATTEMPT #2

"Did he even read it?" I demanded, as Lily snuck into a crouching position behind the tree, the remains of my note in her clenched fist.

She shook her head. "I doubt it. He must've known it was from you, and he must've known what it was about. He really doesn't want to forgive you."

"Told ya."

"Don't give up so soon, Rosie. We can do this, girl."

"How? I think this is the hardest thing I've ever done!"

"That's… sad. I'm not gonna lie. That's just sad."

"*Regardless,* Lily, what do we do now?" I snapped, irritable. "How can I apologize if I can't speak to the person or write them a note?"

"Well, technically you *did* apologize, because you did write him a note," said Lily. "He just didn't read it."

"That doesn't count," I said impatiently. "That's like verbally apologizing to someone who can't hear you. It doesn't count if they don't hear you."

Lily's eyes lit up. "Hear you… that's right, for an apology to count, he just has to *hear* you!"

"Yeah, but how is he going to hear me if he won't let me —"

Lily held up her hand to silence me. She peeked around behind the trunk of the tree, ensuring no passing cars, nearby snooping neighbors, or Rock himself was watching. Then she darted out from behind the tree and began to prowl around Rock's house on tiptoe, appearing to be searching for something. I watched as she disappeared around the corner of the house. Eventually, she slunk back around, grinning.

"I know where it is!" she hissed, slipping back behind the tree and crouching next to me.

"Where what is?"

"His bedroom!"

"His bedroom?" I repeated. "Why do I need to know where his bedroom is?"

"Because it has a window," she said, grinning wickedly, "and for it to count as an apology? He just has to *hear* you."

So I followed her out from behind the tree, around the side of the house, and to the basement window she pointed out.

"Now," she whispered, as we squatted on either side of it, just out of sight, "we have to catch him by surprise. That way he doesn't have time to run away before he hears your apology. I peeked in there earlier and he was just sitting in there talking to some of his plants. Are you ready, Rose?"

I took a deep breath, then nodded. "I'm ready."

"Then show us what you got, girl!"

I cleared my throat, banged on Rock's window, and bellowed, as loudly as I could, *"I'M SORRY I ATE YOUR FAVORITE CHILD!"*

I was scared to sneak a glimpse into the window, feeling my entire body was frozen from the inside out. But cautiously, carefully, I leaned over and peered into the window. Rock was sitting in a waffle chair, facing away from us, with headphones over his ears, nodding his head to the beat and chatting animatedly with a few potted plants on his desk. He hadn't heard me. I groaned.

"Now what?" I asked, turning to Lily.

"What do you mean, *now what?* There's no way he didn't hear that! You apologized and your conscience is clear. Let's get out of here."

"He has headphones on. He didn't hear me!" I protested.

"Whaaat?" Lily peered into the window as well, then echoed my groan. "Ugh, just our luck. He didn't have those on a few minutes ago!"

"Do you have his number?" I asked. "Or do you know anyone who does? We could call him."

"I don't know anybody who has his number," she muttered, crossing her arms like a stubborn child. "This is ridiculous. You just want to apologize. Why does it have to be so hard? Look at us, trying to yell inside windows like a couple of vagrants!"

"I know," I complained. "It's like fate won't let us do it without doing something desperate, almost *dramatic*."

Lily perked up again, turning to me. "Rose… that's it. I know what we can do!"

"What?"

"Something *dramatic*."

CHAPTER FIFTEEN: APOLOGY ATTEMPT #3

Thirty minutes later, Myranda, the Girl Who Eats Paste was crouching behind Rock's house with us, as were several of her garbage-covered, smelly backup singers.

"I was really pleased to get your call, Lily," she said, plucking a used tissue from her hair and throwing it onto the ground. "You're lucky I was able to come on such short notice, though. I am the future —"

"The future world's best singer, yeah, we know," Lily finished impatiently. "Look, for reasons I won't disclose, we might not have much time for Rose to apologize to Rock. So we need to get straight into it, okay? Go ring the doorbell — *hide your backup singers* — and tell Rock's father you're here to sing a song for Rock's birthday."

"What if it's not his birthday?" Myranda asked, frowning.

"Then tell him you're here to sing a song for his father's birthday."

"What if it's not his father's birthday?"

"Then tell him you're here to sing a song for your birthday."

"Why would he want to listen to me sing a song about my own birthday?"

"Wait… is it your birthday?" I asked.

She nodded, and I kind of wanted to laugh, but Lily was getting frustrated.

"Then make something else up! Just tell him you'd like his opinion on your new song. He won't think that's weird, right? I mean, you two are friends, aren't you?"

"Nope. We've never spoken before. I don't think he even knows who I am," Myranda said cheerfully.

This plan was sounding worse and worse with each word Myranda and Lily spoke.

"You know what," I interjected, a sinking feeling in my heart, "maybe we should just forget it. This isn't going to work."

"It's going to work," Lily said firmly. "Why don't you pretend you've secretly had a crush on him for a long time, Myranda, and that you want to express your love to him through singing?"

"The only problem with that," said Myranda, twirling a lock of hair around her finger, "is that I actually *have* had a crush on him for a really long time, and I think if I tell him that, it would totally give it away."

Lily let out an exasperated sigh. "You know what, just sing him a song and hopefully he'll stay and watch out of pure curiosity! All we need is for him to hear what Rose says when she apologizes, after all. So if you can yell loud and fast, Rose, we don't have anything to worry about."

With that, she turned and marched back to our hiding spot behind the thick oak tree, beckoning for me to follow. We hid behind the tree, watching through its branches as Myranda bounded up the steps to ring the doorbell. Her backup singers remained pressed against the side of the house, hidden.

After she'd rung the bell, Lily and I both held our breath. It was a few minutes, as usual, before anyone answered the door. Rock's father now looked annoyed, but he gave Myranda a smile that didn't exactly cover up said annoyance. He was obviously attempting to look polite.

"Can you hear what they're saying?" I asked Lily.

She shook her head.

We watched as Rock's father and Myranda conversed. Then Rock's father turned and walked away, but he'd left the door ajar.

"That's definitely a good sign, isn't it?" I hissed.

Lily nodded in excitement.

My heart leapt with joy at the sight of Rock now appearing in the doorway, pushing the door open wider. He smiled his usual goofy smile at Myranda, looking a bit perplexed as to why she was at his doorstep. Myranda took a deep breath, then, according to our plan, she burst into song:

"We all have special things we love
Things we cannot get enough of
So when something happens to them, we cry
Because it's so hard to say goodbye!"

Right on cue, her backup singers burst out from behind the house, echoing her singing and doing impressive acrobatic dance moves. Rock jumped, clearly not knowing they were there. He looked around, obviously trying to find the source of the music that had also started playing. I didn't know where it was coming from, either.

"There comes a time when we must let go
You cannot hold onto rotten dough
So let's move on now, let's forgive a girl you
know
Who goes by the name of Rose!"

This was my cue. I froze. Lily gave me a hard shove out from behind the tree. I stumbled a little bit, then charged toward the house, yelling, "I'm ate your favorite child, sorry! No, wait, I mean… I'm favorite your child ate, sorry! No, no, wait, I mean…"

The music had stopped, and so had the dancers, everyone staring at me. Myranda and her gang looked unimpressed by my stuttering and stumbling. Lily looked furious that I couldn't get the words right. Rock was gaping at me in a strange mixture of horror and confusion.

Finally, I got the words right. "I'm sorry I ate your favorite child!" I shouted, coming to a stop right next to Myranda on the yard.

Relief washed over me as Rock continued gawking at me. He had heard me. He was looking right at me, he didn't have headphones in, there was no way he hadn't heard my apology. It counted! I'd finally managed to force him to listen to my apology, and now I had apologized to all seven people on the list. Now I could die in peace.

But something still didn't feel right. I watched as the music started back up again and the dancers resumed their dancing, Myranda resuming her singing. Rock seemed to have just figured out why Myranda was there in the first place, to trick him into hearing an apology he didn't want to hear, and he turned and stormed back into the house, slamming the door behind him.

The music faded away. Myranda quieted down. The dancers froze mid-dance moves, some of them in quite awkward positions and losing their balance, toppling over in the grass.

"You did it, Rose!" Lily cheered, running out from behind the tree. She threw her arms around me. I pushed her away.

"He didn't forgive me," I muttered.

Lily sighed in exasperation. "*Rose.* We've gone over this a gajillion times. He doesn't need to forgive you! You apologized, you did your part, you can relax. You're done now. We can celebrate. Wanna get one more ice cream before you explode?"

"Explode?" Myranda echoed, looking at me in terror.

We both ignored her.

"I told you before, Lily! This apology actually meant something to me. Breaking Ellie From Second Grade's coccyx? Not a big deal. Burning Myranda's house down? Who cares? And Trayvon will stop crying eventually. But eating Rock's child? I just can't live with that on my conscience."

"Well, you don't have to live with it much longer. You'll be dead soon enough."

"Lily!"

"Oh, all right." She sighed. "We'll keep trying to get him to talk to you. But how on earth will we do it? He's not going to open the door for anyone now, no matter who we bring. He'll know it's someone we sent, just like Myranda."

My bloated stomach began to burn so badly I had to crawl back behind the oak tree and curl into a ball, hugging my knees to my chest. I had such a terrible headache from stress that I just couldn't deal with it any longer. I almost wanted to explode right then and there just to escape it all. I could hear Lily and Myranda talking over by Rock's house, but I tuned them out. I needed a moment to just forget about the issue and rest.

After a few minutes, Lily came over and squatted next to me behind the tree. "Myranda and I were chatting," she said. "I told her everything. She came up with a really good idea."

"Great," I muttered unenthusiastically, staring at a dead leaf on the ground that probably looked just as lifeless as my own soul. "Let's do it."

"Don't you want to know what it is?" Lily asked.

I didn't have the energy to answer.

She sighed and stood up. "Okay. Myranda and I will go figure everything out. We'll come get you when it's time."

I didn't say anything. She walked away.

CHAPTER SIXTEEN: APOLOGY ATTEMPT #4

The sun was starting to go down by the time Lily returned to my spot behind the oak tree. I hadn't moved. I was so stressed, so dejected, and so exhausted. Lily kept trying to get me to stand up and follow her over to Rock's house, but I just couldn't. Maybe this was the end. Maybe this was what dying felt like. Maybe I was going to explode all over Rock's oak tree, a year after I'd eaten his cactus. The poor guy.

But when I heard voices, I couldn't quell my curiosity. I sat up.

"What do you *want?*" snarled Rock.

I peeked around the thick trunk of the oak tree to see him standing on the front step again, his usual dorky smile gone and a furious expression on his face. Standing in front of him was a group of people. My eyes widened as I realized who they were.

"Myranda came up with the idea after I explained to her everything that was going on and everything that had happened," Lily whispered. "She thought this would work. There is strength in numbers, after all. Come on, let's go over there so we can hear what everyone's saying."

Reluctantly, I allowed her to drag me over to Rock's house. He didn't look at us. Maybe he didn't see us. He was focused on the group of people standing between us.

"Rose Dilfinski has decided to make some important changes in her life, and own up to her past mistakes," Myranda was saying. Her backup dancers nodded in unison. "Look, she apologized to the rest of us, and we all forgave her. Didn't we, guys?"

They all nodded, even Trayvon.

"I was so angry at her when she left my house today," he said. "But it breaks my heart to be angry at people almost as much as it breaks my heart when they criticize sports. So I forgave her."

"And I have to live in a Dumpster now because she burned my house down," Myranda added. "But if I didn't forgive her, the anger would burn my soul into nothingness just like the fire burned my house into nothingness."

"I can see by reading the structure of her facial features that Rose is not wise," Pauline chipped in. "That means she cannot be held entirely accountable for her stupidity. It's just part of who she is. It was written in the stars when she was born."

Ellie started to say something, but had to stop due to a sudden coughing and sneezing fit. Everyone else subtly inched away from her.

"I believe Rose's episodes of acting out are rooted in her desperate need for attention," said Gurpreet in his slow, calm voice. "She was in my office for therapy today, which means she is working to remedy the problem."

"I don't care!" snapped Rock, his face as red as his hair. "She ate Boris! She just picked him up and bit his head off. How would you like it if someone picked you up and took a bite out of your head?"

"It would be quite disturbing, but it would at least be a quick way to die," Myranda said.

Rock glared at her, starting to tremble with rage.

This wasn't going well at all. Dejected, I started to walk away. Lily grabbed my arm and dragged me back.

"Rose is a changed person, Rock," Myranda insisted. "You've got to forgive her.

Look, if you forgive her, I'll give you my autograph… the autograph of the future world's best singer and the *only* singer to ever be raised in a Dumpster… *free of charge.*"

The backup singers gasped. Trayvon looked jealous. Lily snorted and muttered something under her breath.

"No," said Rock. He crossed his arms.

"But it's my birthday, Rock," Myranda pressed. "The thing I want more than anything on my birthday? Is a welcome mat for my Dumpster. But the thing I would want if I couldn't have that? Is for you to forgive Rose."

"Not going to happen," he growled.

"Refusing to forgive someone does more damage to you than the other person, Rock," said Gurpreet softly. "Forgiving Rose is the healthiest thing you can do for yourself."

"Rock," drawled Pauline, stepping forward. "If you do not forgive Rose, you will be doomed to a life of misfortune. It is written in the stars, Rock. Oh, yes, I can see it all… I see you, living in a worse place than a Dumpster… I see you, living in… a *sandbox.*"

"I'd rather live in a sandbox than a Dumpster," he said.

"It is a disgusting sandbox," Pauline continued. "Commonly used for wild animals to relieve themselves. Children make sand castles on your face while you sleep. Spiders and sand bugs crawl into your ears and eat your brain while you are unaware —"

"Rock," Ellie interrupted. "If you do not forgive Rose, I'll come over there and cough all over you and give you tuberculosis —"

"You have tuberculosis?" he spluttered, backing away.

"— and Trayvon will never stop crying because your hatred of Rose just breaks his heart," Ellie finished.

"It does," said Trayvon, sniffling. "It really does. Oh, *why can't everyone just get along???*" He burst into loud, obnoxious sobs, burying his face in his hands.

For a moment, his wails were the only sound. Rock stared at everyone in silence. Then he shot me an icy glare, marched back into his house, and slammed the door.

CHAPTER SEVENTEEN: THE FINAL APOLOGY

It was time for desperate measures. I hadn't wanted it to come down to this. But I did what I had to do. I strode up the walk, up the steps, up to Rock's door. I wrenched it open. Rock stood in his kitchen, glaring at me. The kitchen was full of plants, some big, some small, some funky-shaped, some normal. But I knew that not one of those plants meant as much to him as Boris had.

"I'm dying," I told Rock.

He said nothing. His facial expression did not change.

"I have a rare illness that's going to kill me any second now."

He scoffed. "Oh, yeah? What is this *rare illness?*"

"Flatulentitis."

His eyes widened. "No…" he whispered.

I nodded grimly.

He was quick to recover. "Well, boo hoo. I don't care. Go ahead and die, then. At least you know it's coming. *Boris* didn't. Boris had no idea he was about to be eaten. He saw you coming, someone he had always thought was his *friend,* and he thought you were just picking him up to give him a hug or something, but then you... you..."

Rock burst into tears.

"Rock, I feel really bad. I want to make things right. There's got to be a way I can do that."

"Not unless you can bring Boris back from the dead!" he cried, wiping his tear-stained face.

"Come on, Rock," said Lily, stepping into the kitchen behind me. "Rose is *dying*, and her dying wish is for you to forgive her. Instead of being at home with her family and friends, she's chosen to spend the last few moments of her life with you, apologizing because she hurt you. Doesn't that mean anything to you? Don't you think a human is more important than a plant?"

Rock stopped crying and stared at her for a few seconds. My heart swelled with hope. He seemed to be thinking it over.

"Boris would want you to forgive her," Lily added. "Boris was… um… forgiving."

"Okay," Rock murmured. He turned to me, looking as if he was using up all the self-control he had. Very painfully, as if he could barely bring himself to speak the words, he said, "I forgive you."

I was so overjoyed that I ran across the kitchen and threw my arms around him. To my surprise, he hugged me back… a bit tightly. I felt an immense relief as I let out the loudest, biggest, most explosive fart I had ever emitted in my life… all over the baby spider plant sitting on the table behind me. It immediately wilted, shriveled up, and turned brown.

"NOOOOOOO!" cried Rock, shoving me away. "Lolita! You killed her! She's *dead!*"

But I wasn't paying him any attention. Lily and I were staring at each other, stunned.

"You farted," she whispered. Then, louder — "You *farted!*"

"I'm cured!" I exclaimed, throwing my hands into the air. "I no longer have Flatulentitis!"

We jumped up and down, hugging each other, then raced out of Rock's house, leaving him on his knees sobbing over his lifeless spider plant and leaving the group of curious onlookers

I'd apologized to earlier standing in front of his house in confusion.

"Let's check out of that hotel, get our things, and go home," said Lily. "Oh, this is wonderful. You're not dying anymore! I didn't think there was a cure for Flatulentitis! This is the best moment of my life!"

"Sure is," I said. "Wanna get ice cream?"

"You bet."

And off we went to get ice cream, completely forgetting about the murder I had just committed — the second murder of my life.

EPILOGUE

Our lives got a lot better after that. I guess sometimes you need to be reminded of how beautiful and precious life is, because that's something we as humans tend to forget. We get angry. We get distracted. We get careless. Then something horrible comes along and threatens our lives and we remember what really matters.

I was so happy that I wasn't dying that I began smiling at each person I saw, every single day. I even smiled at strangers and was reported to the police for "suspicious smiling", but I didn't care. My life was so much better now that I could fart again. I was the happiest I'd ever been.

Lily's life got a lot better, too. When we came back home after our journey of going around and apologizing to people, Arthur the robin didn't follow us. We found out he'd been eaten by a snake while waiting for us outside our hotel room window. Lily was so overjoyed not to have a stalker anymore that she got a snake tattoo, to ward off any future robins that may have been considering stalking her.

The only person who didn't seem to be happy after my recovery was Papa P-Rick. When we called and told him I was going to live after all, he was furious. He said he'd already gotten everything ready for that extravagant funeral he'd promised me. He had gotten the pope and the President and even the British prime minister to agree to come, and he'd been planning to borrow some of Myranda's backup dancers.

"Do you even think about other people, Blose?" he snarled at me, before hanging up the phone.

But Lily and I just laughed. Nothing could upset us anymore. I had finally learned something, probably the most important thing a person can learn:

There is truly nothing better than living a joyful life.

Made in the USA
Monee, IL
15 January 2025

76947955R10080